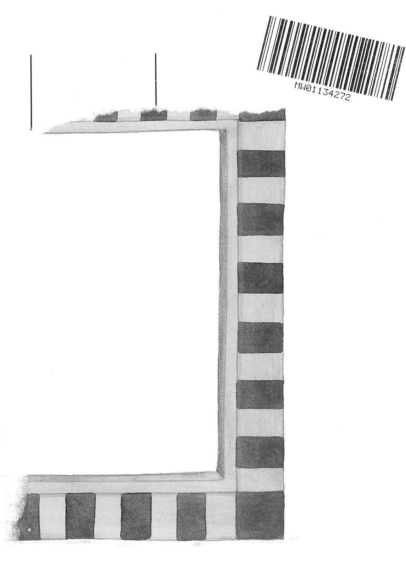

This book belongs to

....

Published by
British Association for Adoption & Fostering
(BAAF)
Saffron House
6-10 Kirby Street
London EC1N 8TS
www.baaf.org.uk

Charity registration 275689 (England and Wales)
and SC039337 (Scotland)

British Library Cataloguing in Publication Data
A catalogue record for this book is available
from the British Library

ISBN 978 1 905664 73 3

Project management by Abi Omotoso, BAAF
Designed and typeset by Helen Joubert Design
Printed in Great Britain by The Lavenham Press Limited
Trade distribution by Turnaround Publisher Services, Unit 3,
Olympia Trading Estate, Coburg Road, London N22 6TZ

BAAF is the leading UK-wide membership organisation for all
those concerned with adoption, fostering and child care issues.

Printed on FSC certified, chlorine-free paper

The Most Precious Present in the World

by Becky Edwards, illustrated by Louise Comfort

The author

Becky Edwards is an award winning children's author who lives in Chichester, West Sussex, with her husband and two children. She was inspired to write *The Most Precious Present in the World* when two of her closest friends adopted young children. Over the years, the comments and feelings of those children have helped Becky to finish the story. Becky is currently the co-ordinator of a children's centre where she spends lots of time working with and talking to children and their families, but whenever she can she escapes to the shed at the bottom of her garden to write stories and daydream.

The illustrator

Louise Comfort began illustrating whilst studying at Kingston University with a regular flow of commissions from Thomas Nelson & Son Publisher and various magazines. This was followed by many educational and activity books for b Small Publishing, Scholastic, Hodder & Stoughton and Dorling Kindersley. In recent years, Louise has illustrated a variety of picture books for Penguin, Walker Books, Egmont and Campbell Books. Louise lives in Lincolnshire with her husband, two young boys and Mr. Bridger, their black Labrador.

To Angel and Carys – my inspiration.
To Ninesh, Mia and Joss –
the most precious presents in my world.
BECKY EDWARDS

To Charlie and Finley.
LOUISE COMFORT

It always takes my mum a very long time to brush my hair.

That's because it's so curly.

Sometimes I wish it wasn't curly, sometimes I wish it was straight, just like my mum's.

But Mum says my hair is beautiful. She says when she was little, she always wanted curly hair just like mine. She says my beautiful, curly hair is a present from my birth mum.

That's because I'm *adopted*.

3

My dad's eyes are as blue as the sky on a sunny day and my mum's are as green and sparkly as the sea.

But my eyes are dark, as dark as the night sky. That's what my dad says.

Mum says my beautiful dark eyes are a present from my birth dad.

That's because I'm *adopted*.

5

And when my mum and dad smile they don't have a dimple on the side of one cheek like I do.

Mum says that's also because I'm adopted. She says the dimple on my cheek is the spot where my birth mum and dad kissed me goodbye.

'Were they sad when they kissed me goodbye?' I asked.

'Very sad,' Mum said.

'Is that why they gave me those presents? Were my curly hair and my dark eyes goodbye presents?'

'Your birth mum gave you your beautiful hair because it is like her hair and your birth dad gave you your beautiful dark eyes because they are like his eyes. And Mia, part of them will always be part of you. They gave you your dimple because they wanted you to remember that they will always love you. Just like Dad and I do.'

I sat on my mum's lap and we read a story and I drew a picture of me and my mum and dad. I drew me with lots and lots of curly hair.

Mum said it looked just like us. She stuck it on the fridge door next to the picture of me on my new bike, the one that Mum and Dad gave me for my birthday.

Getting presents is very exciting!

'Mum,' I said, 'my birth mum and dad gave me lots of presents: my hair and my eyes and my dimple, but they didn't give you or Dad anything. Didn't they like you?'

My mum stopped sticking my picture on the fridge. She came and sat down next to me and gave me a great big hug.

'They gave your dad and me the most precious present in the world,' she said.

'More precious than your sparkly earrings from Dad?' I asked.

Mum nodded.

'Even more precious than your party shoes or the new handbag that you bought for cousin Rachel's wedding?'

Mum smiled.

'Much more precious than all those things,' she said. 'They gave us YOU.'

'Me!' I said, 'I'm a present?'

Mum nodded. 'A very special present.'

'Are some of my friends presents too?' I asked.

'All children are presents for their mums and dads when they are born,' my mum said. 'But you are extra special because you were two presents. You were a present for your birth dad and your birth mum *and* you were a present for Dad and me.'

Being two presents is very confusing, so I got down from Mum's lap and she made us both some hot chocolate with lots of squirty cream and marshmallows to help us think.

I fetched my spoon with the cat handle and stirred and stirred until all the marshmallows had melted.

'Didn't my birth mum and dad want to keep me?' I asked in a quiet voice. 'I always want to keep my presents.'

My mum stopped drinking her hot chocolate and sat me on her lap.

'They wanted to keep you very much,' she said, stroking my curly hair, 'but they loved you so much, that most of all they wanted to keep you safe and happy.
And they knew they couldn't do that.
So they did something very special.
They gave you to Dad and me.'

'Did they wrap me up in shiny paper?' I asked. Mum laughed.

'No, not in shiny paper, darling,' she said, 'you were wrapped in your blue and yellow star blanket and you were wearing a red hat. And as soon as Dad and I held you, we knew. We knew it was you we had been waiting for, for such a long, long time. And then you opened your deep, dark eyes and smiled your beautiful smile and it seemed as though you knew it too.'

'I think I did know it too,' I said.

And I touched my mum's smooth, straight hair and gave her a great big hug.

15

Sometimes I wish I wasn't adopted.
Sometimes being adopted is very hard.
Sometimes it makes me feel confused.
Sometimes it makes me feel sad.
And sometimes it makes me feel very cross.

But Mum says that's OK.

She says it's alright to feel confused and sad. She says it's
even OK to feel very cross because being adopted isn't easy.
And then she hugs me and strokes my curly hair and reads
me my favourite stories until Dad comes home.

18

And when Dad comes home, he kisses me on the tip of my nose and wraps me in my blue and yellow star blanket and twirls me round and round.

'Hello sweetheart, I've been waiting all day to see you again,' he smiles.

I look into his eyes, as blue as the sky on a sunny day, and I touch the star blanket that I was wrapped in when I arrived.

And I feel very special.

Because...

Being adopted makes me special.

Being adopted means I was two presents when I was born.

Being adopted makes me the most precious present in the world.